Accumulated Lessons in Displacement

"Poring over this collection, I find manifested a familiar equanimity, a deep bass note of joy upholding the heart despite the many and serial griefs and other displacements (both internal and external) that human life appears to require of us along the journey. I find—as I attend—that the speaker has previously attended with great devotion to the persons, places, and things that have accompanied both her journey and her many, many remarkable sojourns along the way. Because she has refused to squander her accumulated lessons, the reader is also mentored toward wisdom, grace, and peace."

—**Scott Cairns**, author of *Slow Pilgrim: Collected Poems*

"Hicks invites readers to travel with her from Singapore to Baltimore, from Amman to the Congo. The contemplations here are not mere travel reflections; instead, they explore, as Hicks says, 'the small balls of hope' that insist themselves and help us to be present with personal and global suffering. Richly rooted in wisdoms from many traditions, these poems remind us that the paradoxes we all live with are as much gift as burden."

—**Jennifer Wallace**, author of *Almost Entirely*

"Tautly written and closely observed, Rachel Hicks's debut collection crackles with energy and insight. While taking the reader from the Chesapeake Bay to Southwestern China, the true movement in these meticulously rendered poems is ever inward, an interior journey bursting with bright sadness and bitter joy. This is a volume to revisit and savor."

—**Brian Volck**, author of *Attending Others*

"Rachel Hicks, a global nomad, clearly perceives the nuanced natural world, its light and shadow, birdsong and rain, and the unseen world in all its mystery and complexity. This pilgrim is both at home and searching for a home. If you 'wander unknown,' may Hicks's verses serve as an 'astonishing little altar,' built by her own gifted and 'benevolent hand' to 'point the way.'"

—**Susan Delaney Spear**, author of *On Earth . . .*

"With sharp imagery, gorgeous language, and hard-fought wisdom, *Accumulated Lessons in Displacement* is a gift from a truly attentive poet. Through personal narratives and meditations on biblical themes, Rachel Hicks takes readers on a journey of longing and belonging. These poems are a beautiful reminder of what it means to live as faithful pilgrims in a world that is both harrowing and hope-filled: 'we come to see each scene / as something to inhabit, and we wake // to more than mortals, wake to mysteries.'"

—**Whitney Rio-Ross**, author of *Birthmarks*

Accumulated Lessons in Displacement

Poems

BY
Rachel E. Hicks

RESOURCE *Publications* · Eugene, Oregon

ACCUMULATED LESSONS IN DISPLACEMENT
Poems

Copyright © 2025 Rachel E. Hicks. All rights reserved. Except for brief quotations in critical publications or reviews, no part of this book may be reproduced in any manner without prior written permission from the publisher. Write: Permissions, Wipf and Stock Publishers, 199 W. 8th Ave., Suite 3, Eugene, OR 97401.

Resource Publications
An Imprint of Wipf and Stock Publishers
199 W. 8th Ave., Suite 3
Eugene, OR 97401

www.wipfandstock.com

PAPERBACK ISBN: 979-8-3852-4692-2
HARDCOVER ISBN: 979-8-3852-4693-9
EBOOK ISBN: 979-8-3852-4694-6

VERSION NUMBER 06/24/25

Unless otherwise noted, all scriptures are from the KING JAMES VERSION, public domain.

For Jim

We will bear whatever troubles come;
we will share whatever joys God gives us.

Contents

Acknowledgments | xi

Sojourn | 1

Bright Sadness, Bitter Joy
The Exile Speaks of Mountains | 4
Remnants of Empire | 6
Birth of the Girl-Child | 7
First Kiss | 9
Philoxenia | 11
Cameo | 12
Disaster Chaplaincy Training | 13
The Hill Above Minamisanriku | 15
An Initiation to Ash Wednesday | 17
Hospitality | 18
The Coveted Gift | 19
High Winds on the Chesapeake Bay Bridge | 20
Old Job | 22
Depression, Annotated | 24
Come Kneel | 26
It Wasn't Odd | 27
Visit to Sarajevo | 28
You Kept Trying to Say *Butter* | 30
A Father's Plea | 31
Accumulated Lessons in Displacement | 32
Gift | 35
Respite Walk | 36
Under the Broom Tree | 37

Bright Sadness | 38
Kou 口 | 39
A Voice Is Heard in Ramah | 40
Uninventable | 41
Jury Duty | 42
The Morning After Freddie Gray's Funeral | 43
Melancholy | 45
The Wood Is Dry | 46

A Deeper Knowing

Quiddity | 50
Just Before | 51
The Truth about the River | 52
Dream | 53
Walk to Emmaus | 54
Mali at Ramadan | 56
By Degrees | 57
Metanoia | 58
Allegory | 59
This Givenness | 60
One Unused to Ashes | 62
It Is Happening Now (I) | 64
It Is Happening Now (II) | 65
Post Miracle (I) | 66
Post Miracle (II) | 68
The Interior | 70
Chengdu Pastoral | 72
Cicadas, East of Eden | 73
A Prayer: On Synthetic Snowflakes | 75
Acedia | 76
Everything Is a Departure | 78
Cairn at West Clear Creek | 80
Clarification | 81
Speak Like Rain | 83

Late Discovery | 84
Roundtop Ski Lodge | 85
Cusp | 86
Gravity and Grace | 87
Late February | 88
My Daughter Asks for a Pomegranate | 89

Notes | 91
About the Poet | 95

Acknowledgments

Grateful acknowledgment is made to the following journals in which certain poems, sometimes in slightly different iterations, are forthcoming or first appeared.

America Magazine: "Clarification" and "Dream"

Anglican Theological Review: "Respite Walk"

Bloodstone Review: "Everything Is a Departure"

Ekstasis Magazine: "A Prayer: On Synthetic Snowflakes" and "An Initiation to Ash Wednesday"

Fare Forward: "My Daughter Asks for a Pomegranate"

Gulf Stream Literary Magazine: "Chengdu Pastoral"

Little Patuxent Review: "The Exile Speaks of Mountains"

Off the Coast: "The Coveted Gift"

Pen In Hand: "Hospitality," "Remnants of Empire," and "Birth of the Girl-Child"

Presence: A Journal of Catholic Poetry: "By Degrees"

Relief: A Journal of Art and Faith: "It Wasn't Odd" and "Just Before"

Spiritus: "Quiddity"

St. Katherine Review: "Cameo"

The Baltimore Review: "Accumulated Lessons in Displacement"

The Penwood Review: "Cicadas, East of Eden"

The Windhover: "Disaster Chaplaincy Training"

Tiger's Eye Journal: "Speak Like Rain"

Vita Poetica: "Walk to Emmaus"

Welter: "The Truth About the River"

"By Degrees" was nominated for a Pushcart Prize in 2023

"Quiddity" was a Finalist in the New York Encounter Poetry Contest, 2022, and was nominated for a Pushcart Prize

"My Daughter Asks for a Pomegranate" won Third Place in the *Fare Forward* Poetry Competition, 2022

"The Exile Speaks of Mountains" was the Runner Up in the Enoch Pratt Library Poetry Contest, 2018

"Birth of the Girl-Child" won Second Place in the Maryland Writers Association Annual Poetry Competition, 2016

I owe immense gratitude to all my family, friends, and fellow writers who encouraged me in creating this collection. Jim, I may not have taken more than a step or two down the path of becoming a poet and writer were it not for your loving support and practical help. Early on in our marriage, you saw the spark of life writing gave me, and you helped me, in each season of our lives, to carve out time and space to write, read, and gather with others called to this vocation. You considered my poetry vital and valuable, and in doing so, you helped me also to see it as such.

You've always been my biggest cheerleader. Collin and Jackie, thank you for sharing your joy with me over even early drafts, letting me write about you, and being the kind of humans who see poetry as essential to life. Many thanks to my parents, my brother, and my in-laws for being early readers of some drafts, and for believing in my work even when words or phrases required occasional unpacking.

A big thank-you to my beta readers and fellow poets Brian Volck, Lisa Toth Salinas, Jennifer Wallace, and Susan Delaney Spear. I am honored by the time, care, and thought you put into considering this manuscript and giving me your honest and helpful feedback. I believe the collection is stronger because of your help. I would also like to thank my poetry critique friends, Christine Stewart and Clare Banks—you helped me to craft many early drafts in this collection, asking insightful questions and helping me to consider form and find new ways to approach subjects. My copy editor (and fellow poet), Evan Rhoades, was a delight to work with and helped me to tighten up each poem. I am indebted to fellow poets and teachers from poetry workshops I've attended—particularly Scott Cairns, from whom I learned much about interrogating each line to see that it does its required work in opening up meaning and possibility. Finally, and most importantly, I'm grateful to God for allowing me a poetic vocation. *Soli Deo gloria.*

Sojourn

Our days on earth are like a shadow—
we wander unknown. Light slashes through
in temporal bands, dappled, concealing.
There is no abiding; only shape-
shifting, partial sight. Each heart must bear
its own bitterness, and no one may
share its joy.
              There is no abiding—
sometimes this is mercy: weariness
settles, even over a good life,
a grateful heart. *The longer I live . . .*
the old saints say, until they go quiet.
Only their eyes—gentle, wounded—speak
and heal us, fractionally, as we
come alongside. Where they go, we can't
yet follow—
              how we long to follow!
The fullness awaits. This flagging faith.
We see each other dark. Shadowlands.
Not yet what we shall be—light, and home.

Bright Sadness, Bitter Joy

*Is it foolish to speak of little joys that occur in the middle of tragedy?
It is our humanity. Whatever we have left of it.
We must not deny it to ourselves.*

~ *ILYA KAMINSKY*

The Exile Speaks of Mountains

In the Himalayan foothills during the monsoons
the electricity once stayed off for fifteen days.
Every morning there was chai with sugar cubes

and buffalo milk, delivered to our kitchen door
in tin carafes strapped with thick ropes to a mule.
We kept warm by feeding the stove log after log

and entertained by watching our spit sizzle
on its tin top. My brother held my hand on the trail
to and from school, scanning for leopard scat

or thieving langur monkeys in the trees.
I write this from my brick colonial in Baltimore,
decades removed, drinking black tea with cream and sugar—

the heat of exile churning in my blood.
I drive an SUV, shop at Target, and fight tears
at random moments, like when I open the door

of the Punjab store down on 33rd, suddenly and viscerally
at home among the turmeric and cardamom, Neem soaps,
and steaming samosas under foil on the counter,

while the kind owner offers a mango juice box
to my daughter. Only if I embrace this life
as a perpetual pilgrim do I find solace in remembering

the terraced cemetery in the Himalayan pines
where the mute woman and her donkey guard the graves,
the distant beat of tabla drums, the bounce

of our flashlights on the trail walking home at night,
the thrill of leopards in the dark, the high peak
of Bandarpunch to the north, glowing in moonlight.

Remnants of Empire

I left the snake coiled under my sheet—
a toy, but lifelike enough
to snap blood through your aging veins

like a starter's pistol, to yank
a garbled scream from your lips
when you came in to make my bed.

By lunch, I'd forgotten—returned
to muttered streams of abuses,
thick air, stewing hurt.

I shrank, deflected—*An accident,
so sorry, ayah*. But you knew;
brought me a sandwich

of chili peppers hidden
in folds of cheese and ham.
I ate my penance silently.

In your small rooms
in Old Delhi, your grown son
hacked at a cobra slithering in

the open drain. You'd told me;
I'd forgotten. My tongue sears still
with remembrance.

Birth of the Girl-Child

> "Raising a daughter is like watering your neighbor's garden."
> Traditional Indian proverb

When she emerges in blood and mucus,
the birthing room steeps in quiet fury.

Husband twitches, aghast,
when told through the curtain,

disappears into the yawning twilight,
oncoming dark, scent of drought.

On the pallet, knuckles against teeth,
wife is silent, freshly emptied.

Already she's dodged the fire
in mother-in-law's eyes and hands

for insufficient dowry—now
this girl. She trembles, foresees

how rivers will run dry
and dust choke and strangle

the mechanisms of the turning world
because of the disappeared; thinks

*The earth is sodden with our secrets,
with the blood of our beliefs.*

Mother-in-law squats beside the pail,
which is sufficiently deep.

And the drought is already in the seed
and in the breast.

First Kiss

When my daughter asks me this evening
about my first kiss, I'm silenced.

Singapore, 1985, the Westin Hotel—riding alone
in an elevator, eight years old—too young

to recognize a lecherous smile.
I press B instead of L—think the busboy

on a smoke break is coming to help.
I open my mouth to ask, and it's swallowed up

in fat, wet lips that linger, enjoying my immobile shock.
And it's a red kiss, siren red, full of smoke—

a where's-your-daddy-little-girl kiss.
He backs away slowly, grinning pork chops.

I stumble backwards into the elevator, pushing
any button higher than this.

Jeering laughter fades as the doors close
and I rise. I want to keep riding in that quiet rush

of movement, eyes closed, because already
my gut knows when the doors open again

I will walk out someone else,
someone emptier and heavier

because of what was taken, and given.

This is not what she's asking for.
She waits, hugging a small giggle to her body,

so I choose instead:
Jamal, my seventh-grade crush,

the kiss requested, and given, on a rooftop in Amman
under billions of stars.

Philoxenia

At the end of my departure lounge row,
a man hangs his shaggy head as he waits
to board, cups a bandaged hand against him.
Weary from travel, roots dangling again,
I resist imagining the source of
his pathos, this stranger's extra baggage.
But I can't help myself: perhaps he cut
his finger to the bone chopping onions
for anniversary soup—her favorite—
chopped until she swept into the kitchen,
wearing a bright smile, and purposely laid
her gold ring down, and sashayed out again,
forever. He never ceased the rhythm
of the chop-chop-chop until the steel sliced
sweetly into flesh. Now he waits to board;
under pinkening gauze pulses the wound
that seems to bleed and bleed. It's as I feared:
right in the midst of this sequestered crowd,
I want to cup him against me and sit,
both disheveled, in a kind of silence.

Cameo

You hold a ready lens to each scene and verse,
waiting for yourself to come into focus: you're Joseph—
Judases for brothers, final recompense for your hurts—

or Moses—eyes searching watery walls you've stepped between
for shadow creatures, fissures, but on you walk, aware of trust,
scanning for evidence of God in the seams—

or perhaps an exile returning from Babylon—the crust
of years falling from you, the shofar sounding its jubilant note
as the last foundation stone settles in the dust.

Yet what if you are not the favored son, but one who woke
from dreams, number twelve in line for your father's attentions,
trafficked for debt or indifferent profit, smote

by an obscure hand, no dancing exodus;
rather, death by your stripes in the shadows of a limestone
mausoleum, born one generation too early for deliverance?

What if exile makes such bitter work of your bones
and brittle heart, that the others must kiss you and depart
to witness the stones' rebirth, while you remain alone?

The initial taste of meekness stings acidic, tart
as you accommodate yourself to your bit part.

Disaster Chaplaincy Training

Loiter with intent (in steel-soled boots
when necessary), our instructor tells us.

Partially blind from weeks
of Ground Zero asbestos, she says:

Hover approachably in the aftermath.
Learn to be present in suffering—

acclimate to its pungency—
its yellow, acrid scent.

Sit with victims in their grief and shock
on the broken curb, under a tarp, if available.

Distribute cups of water—
this is your spiritual service.

Perception of safety is critical.
Let kids solve puzzles. Restore balance

with simple questions: what color
was your house?

You are midwives birthing new realities,
she says—everything has changed.

Let them see you cupping a small ball
of hope—toss it up, catch it.

Finally: Nouwen calls us wounded
healers. Know your own tipping point.

Don't let their story become your story.
Hydrate.

The Hill Above Minamisanriku

      Japan Tsunami, 2011

We watch her run slowly up the hill,
her rolled nylons weighing her ankles.

She's lost a shoe—turns,
sees corrugated roofs colliding,

just below her, the devouring sea
almost at her feet.

She needs claws like this monster
to pull herself out of its reach.

She drops her leather handbag,
shudders at its shapeless corpse

behind her on the path, where
a spire plunges point-first

into the vein of the trail. Fear
slows her steps; she runs as if through

dream water, churning and swelling
behind her. We see her gasps,

too small to be heard, watch her
on our phone screens from the hill

above Minamisanriku, recording
the minutes it takes for the city

to die. We shift our screens,
edging her out of the frame.

An Initiation to Ash Wednesday

I don't know how to carry another's
dashed hopes, let alone my own. What new need
presses, sending me abruptly on my
first Lenten journey? I rest the vacuum
against the wall, hurry on with my coat
and hat, minutes late to Mass. I forget
to genuflect when taking my seat. This
sudden succumbing feeds on the glitter
of gold, superfluity of candles,
sacro-heat, the purple-draped, bruised body
above, and the silver urn of ashes—
last year's Palm Sunday fronds scorched, ground to ash
and hidden away until this moment
in which we bear the weight of each other's
burned hosannas, dusty prayers—some answered,
some not. I don't know how to carry this:
another's dashed hopes, let alone my own.

After the comfort of the priest's thick thumb
upon my forehead, the signature of
Jesus—which I will bear till sundown—weighs
so little I almost forget it's there.

Hospitality

Sichuan, China

In the lean-to kitchen, the farmer's wife
juliennes and crushes, shivers of onion
flying from the blade, steam meeting
cold mist at the open door.
I thrust booted feet at the tin
of hot coals under the table outside
and wait, wondering how many
spontaneous meals have serviced me
in my wanderlusting? How much
ambrosial heat, sear and spice,
plumping bulgar and pitted peach?

It seems to be our needful thing
to forage for the magic within our reach—
the translucent rice grains,
the flesh of all creatures griddled or charred,
the way we wonder if nourishment exists
in snapdragons, the cathaya's winged seed—
all the tastes we haven't dared.
And we wonder if the damp earth still
has secrets to disclose that could remain
wondrous and unstained even by our knowing,
our prodding and splitting
with the knife or the tongue.

She emerges balancing three dishes
on outstretched arms and sets them
on the table, shrinking back in pleasure
and gesturing with a gentle turn of hand:
Eat! It's just a little something.

The Coveted Gift

Last month I was given an abrupt gift,
wrapped in white linen and delivered, word
by gentle word, by my doctor and his
weary eyes:
        two months to live, give or take.
It stared at me—innocent as only
death can be.
        And that was the moment when
the life-breath of every created thing
lifted me on hushed, thick wings, helping me
to cast my scream upon the wide waters—
I have all the world to give!

        Now, instead,
I am going the way of all the earth,
empty-handed; but you—even now!—show
your splayed palm, while your other fist clenches
tight, kneads a bruise in the small of your back.
Your concealed palm sweats with unspecified
guilt, hiding the gift I coveted: you.

Suddenly I find I'm lacking nothing—
I'm a cup running over with pity.

High Winds on the Chesapeake Bay Bridge

> On Buechner's "The Magnificent Defeat"

Theories of ruin only take one so far.
Western enthusiasm for the age of a thing
doesn't extend to the body

(steel bodies, perhaps—like this one I keep steady,
ascending the bridge whose ice-crusted girders
jettison into a glass sky—but not flesh).

I think on this as the wind buffets hard
and I make minute corrections
every few seconds to hold course.

How do I find myself here—near dawn,
alone, suspended, hip touched like Jacob's,
creep of arthritis at the hollow—

and what force is this contending with mine
on the long bridge with low guardrails and only
one direction in which to go?

Does this wrestler have a face,
and is it *a face of love, one half-ruined
with suffering and fierce with joy,*

the face a man flees down all the darkness
of his days until at last he cries out
I will not let you go unless you bless me?

The western edge is trimmed in winter gold;
seagulls line rim after rim of hoar-frosted salt,
anchored by thin claws in the gale.

So, the far shore promises small relief,
just a slight dying of the wind;
and I realize I want—what, precisely?

Mostly I want someone—believing—
to sign the cross over me as I go.

Old Job

These are twilight years
I once hoped I'd never see.

Take today: kisses on each cheek
from laughing beauties—

my daughters; gently
rippling sky, high clouds.

Yet the skin around these scars
pulls and itches, flares red;

a cyclone of dust by the well
this morning stole my breath,

seized me—
everything slowed.

Inside I'm cold—
I barely speak to my wife, remembering.

Beneath my bed, a heavy box
laden with silver and gold—

gifts from family and friends
who came after the double portion—

useless currency. My God!
Remove the ice, the burn,

the smell of ash that clings to me.
Some things have healed; everything

is altered. I can commit myself
to no one but you.

Depression, Annotated

I find my words
in bondage to decay:
fingers dance the grapevine
across keys, dyslexifying
word after word until
farther becomes *rafter*, until I write
ti's noly owrds wanyay.

I pause in my urgent, nameless
tasks, again and again,
and wonder what work
my hands ought to be doing.
Forgetting, I make rice
and lentils and read Auden—
which suddenly feels
most urgent of all.

Pages of days and months
turn, meals cold on the tongue,
each alike as prayers—
and still I'm unable to catch
what is being offered, or
am unwilling to give
what is required.

Inertia clouds the thick
minutes of each day—
four of them pass right now
while I tap my sandal against
my heel, sitting in a blue chair
in a still, warm room.

Tonight, the frightened bird
inside my chest batters hard
against its cage.

Come Kneel

Tonight I need the prayer that you would pray.
It's no surprise my wellspring has run dry.
I know that you won't judge these tears and sighs;
my words were spent before yet half this days-

long night had left me broken, soul bereft
of ease or breath, or numbness at the least.
This body cannot worship now, or feast.
I need you, friend, to enter in this cleft

of rock with me and feel this cold, this flint
on every side, this scrape wherever I turn.
And still the sun—it finds me and it burns
to ashes every prayer I mouthed. I sinned

somehow—I must have, but yet no—that's not
his way—not always, is it? No—he prays
for me; he comes himself in hidden rays,
in body shining here, in you. So what

are we to make of that? I know you feel
yourself unworthy to the task, but here
you are, and here am I, and he is near.
I need you, friend—come kneel with me. Come kneel.

It Wasn't Odd

Last night I dreamed my elderly neighbor
sought me out, found me upstairs in my bedroom.
Ms. Dinty—her trademark black baseball cap,
gold-crowned teeth flashing a grimace this time,

not her mischievous smile—climbed into the bed
I had just vacated in surprise, remarked
on its warmth in the early light. *I'm dying*,
she said, shivering. *It's coming now, baby.*

I hovered, then climbed in beside her,
wrapped my arms around her, whispered
How do you know? Maybe I didn't ask
her aloud. She just breathed in, then out.

Because it was a dream it wasn't odd
that the two of us lay there warming,
silent, unafraid. That I wanted this
to be how she was ushered on.

Visit to Sarajevo

In Mount Trebević Park we settle in plastic chairs
at an outdoor café, order beer and snacks.

Dragan chain smokes, jumbles his reminiscing with jokes,
warns my kids off-hand not to stray from the paths

just in case: the mines should be all cleared by now,
but better to be cautious.

When he's fortified, we drive to the city's edge,
where the tunnel's mouth opens toward the hills.

He balks at the entrance fee—ridiculous that one would pay
to enter "*The Sarajevo War Tunnel, House of the Kolar Family*

Salvation During the War, Memory for Peace."
He shows us his fourth-floor apartment with pockmarked façade

where his father still lives, alone,
where Dragan pulled up floor boards for fuel.

We wait for him to mention the friend he saw shot in the head—
which street? A ghost hovers until we know he won't.

At this intersection he boarded the refugee bus.
At this intersection the archduke was shot.

*"On this place Serbian criminals in the night of 25th–26th August 1992
set on fire national and university's Library of Bosnia and Herzegovina*

*Over 2 millions of books, periodicals and documents vanished in the flame.
Do not forget. Remember and warn!"*

Amidst old-town market souvenir shops he takes my arm
in a haze of pride, nostalgia, nightmare—

jumps when firecrackers explode
signaling the end of the Ramadan fast.

"The night before was just like this—no warning.
You never could imagine."

You Kept Trying to Say *Butter*

    for Bozana

But I couldn't
    understand you.

Then we laughed
    together till we

couldn't say
    anything.

My sister, my
    friend—I wish

we could speak
    together

easy in your
    mother tongue.

A Father's Plea

> Luke 15:29–31

We joked in the barley field, side by side
and merry at harvest.

This rag cooled each of our foreheads in turn
when fever struck.

Think of the long slant of sun behind the house
where we rinse off the day's dirt.

Or the clasp of our hands at Shabbat prayer,
the same roughness of skin.

That night half the herd was slaughtered by lions—
remember? We wept together.

What is this talk—you slaved for me?
All that is mine is yours.

Accumulated Lessons in Displacement

I. Home

My bed groaned each night as it received my body
in the dark. My coffee cup was yellow enamel.

Late afternoon sun illuminated the window seat,
the perpetual dust on the houseplant.

My home knew me as I knew it.
No footpath exists leading back to these things.

II. Solace

In exile there is a strange solace—I would never ask for it,
yet here it is: in my brother's grip as he holds my face,

his desperate kiss on my cheek, the green threads
of my sweater on barbed wire, tracing my path

across miles and miles; in the camps where we wait,
each day a misery and a marvel, each person also.

III. Story

My story is singular: my son collected bullet casings
along the way out—made a necklace for his sister under a tarp.

The day we left, the charred pages of my diary
fluttered all around the living room, where a shell

had just blown out the wall. The dancing pages
made a strange poem in my heart.

IV. Language

I was unable to speak for many days.
Natural expressions, gestures—I lost this language.

No one understood, perhaps not even my wife.
I let silence have its way: germination was occurring.

I took this on faith. Not everyone can.
Hope is not a virtue—it happens, or it doesn't.

V. Welcome

In the terminal, a friend waited, embraced me.
To him I was still of abundant use in this world—

the witty professor who always spoke *le mot juste*.
I clung to his arm, wept silently as we walked out

through the door, into a city night that pulsed and spun.
It felt like rebirth.

VI. Grief

When at last I could speak, I let sorrow name itself—
the bitter and the sweet. My wife winced,

changed the subject; my children clasped my hand.
I was trying to learn the word for joy

that settles awkwardly in grief's nest, an oversized bird.
I didn't want to scare it away.

VII. Purpose

There is purpose in displacement—I feel this deeply.
I don't know what it is yet. My wife's tears, my own,

are larger, wetter; our laughter round and warm;
the tread of my shoes, brim of my hat—these sensate things

bring such pleasure. It has to do with magnification—
with being sure that I am alive.

VIII. Remembrance

Sometimes I look back, walk slowly, linger where necessary.
It makes no sense that a soldier can press a button

and somewhere a baby ignites into flame.
And he goes home and brushes his teeth.

What we do to each other, to other created souls.
Always I carry this burden, like a child on my hip.

Gift

Each Sunday in winter
we walk home from church,

ginko leaves sticking to the wet pavement
and the bottoms of our shoes,

past Xiao Liang, who sits on a small
plastic stool outside her fruit shop

slicing pineapple hides with deft strokes.
We buy four wedges on sticks

and she presses several walnuts
into my daughter's eager hands—

who would not eat walnuts
but for this weekly gift.

Respite Walk

My body can walk as far as I want it to.
My child cries behind glass.

I kneel beside this urban stream
flushing plastic and toxins toward the bay;

it is sufficient, banks greening in early spring.
Ripple of water. Fatigue deep in my bones.

I press into my body's memory this moment:
dandelions and buttercups brush my ankles;

forsythia, magnolia explode Easter-like all around.
What seems fitting: sacrament, prayer, oil.

When I return, I must somehow lift the veil—
show her the holy water of our collected tears.

Under the Broom Tree

What is man
that you are mindful of him?

Look away
and let me catch my breath.

Sometimes I wish
there were not so much at stake.

Bright Sadness

In the car yesterday, returning from
another fruitless medical visit,
my daughter kept crying out, gasping in
sharp, inscrutable pain—her synapses
misfiring again and again—and I
don't know why but what suddenly flew from
my lips was, *Turn your cries into opera!*

Her face froze mid-moan; she narrowed her eyes,
struck dumb. Then, the hint of a forgotten
smile hovered at the corners of her mouth.
She belted a long, plaintive note from some
deep reserve, hidden, untapped. It rose and
fell and rose again. Her strong contralto
carried us on its undulating back
the whole way home, and we—just picture it!—
joy-laughed, even while her fingernails pierced
the seat cushion, and mine the steering wheel.

Kou 口

An open mouth.
Hunger.

One letter off
from *koi*—orange

fleshy hole sucks
at water's surface.

Think also
pleading bird beak

blind caw,
clamor

rising din—
feed it again.

Ji kou ren—
literal translation:

How many mouth-people,
your household?

A Voice Is Heard in Ramah

>   On the massacre of the innocents

Tonight, shushing my son's fevered whispers—
his cheeks hot, lips pushed out in a sulky kiss—
the tremors and shades of his first illness
grip me. Thunder is distant on the hills.

This, too, shall pass. Then, in the pregnant dark,
a chucking softly at a mule: Joseph from next door—
his son a month younger than mine—
slips his family through the swallowing dark.

Going where, at this hour, and in haste?
A hot, soft hand grabs for mine and I kiss and kiss
it in the punctuated night. To quell
the strange fire licking at my nerves.

I hush, *Sleep, my son. Sleep to the distant
drum of thunder, of many horses' hooves.*

Uninventable

Somehow it doesn't sound comfortingly Zen
when you say life is in the losing,

but I'll admit, there's a bit of yin and yang
in how artfully you pair unity with diversity.

You despise every offering that doesn't come broken.
We hate to come empty-handed.

(Nobody could make this stuff up.)

Your MVPs are the dispossessed.
You say they'll inherit the whole shebang.

You tell us: give away your shirt. Love your enemy.
Forgive your no-good sister, times infinity.

Pick up your electric chair and follow.

Even though you speak in metaphor,
you seem to mean it.

Jury Duty

I imagined the Quiet Room
for jurors to be overflowing,
but when a migraine sent me
through the labyrinth of Baltimore's
civic courthouse seeking it, I entered
a dim room, perhaps only twenty people,
almost all white. Why?
A large fan, deep couches, a set-apart aura.
Strange guilt rose in me—
but the dim lighting, cool breeze,
fewer hot bodies were all a balm
to my aching head.

I want to decide a case.
I don't want to decide a case.

The Morning After Freddie Gray's Funeral

    Baltimore

In the garden, shears in hand,
I practice murmuring at the mint.
Schools are closed today

and I am bleached of words.
Last night my kids stayed up late
watching pockets of the city blaze—

afraid, self-righteous, perplexed.
My words failed: *yes, but—* and *not that simple.*
I have no ready language for this—

they've never had to know.
The mint's prolific tentacles creep
a half-inch below the topsoil, tangled

and thriving in city soil. It's too much.
I cut it back, try to contain it
in a corner. Cut enough sprigs

for a gallon of tea, enough to share
with Ms. Dinty next door, or Ms. Janet
on the right—as what? An offering, apology?

A way to say I'm trying—learning
about all that fuels these fires still
smoldering this hushed morning?

In the kitchen, mint and black tea leaves
mingle, staining the clear water
irrevocably, which, at least, seems right.

Melancholy

Always a longing—marrow deep—for home,
even when knowing by heart I've never
been there before. It must be the Irish
in me: the throat's lump of yearning that swells
on the third day in a row of lead skies,

the comfort of a lonely wind, its wail
when all else is silence. There's something in
the thin places, the gauzy veil between
here and there, visible, invisible.
I feel this as I get older. Longing

grows—for the hidden life, the glade, the glen,
the hand of silence cupping me; for mist,
a thicker green, a cottage, gray stones, rest,
moss and ferns, water from a cloistered spring.

Always looking back to Eden, forward
to the City with the trees—the ones with
golden leaves for our healing. Early on,
we'll go sit on that bank from time to time,
when the melancholy pricks. And the leaves—

the golden leaves—will heal, refresh, reknit,
console. Perhaps a time will come when we
no longer need them. We can leave them, then,
for others, newly arrived.

The Wood Is Dry

In the greenness of your coming
the pulse of life flowed sweetly through our veins.
You humaned us to feel something:
alive and open to the world again.
We felt, each one, a shock, undone—
yet known and priceless all the same.

In the green time of your coming
the conflagration seemed so far away.
We joined the dance, the lame running,
the newly dead raised fresh again to day.
(Your sorrow words we barely heard—
you puzzled us along your way.)

The day the axe was put to root,
a bitter wind swept down the mountainside.
*Don't weep for me now when the wood
is green; what will you do when it is dry?*
You shriveled, parched; we simply watched.
Our hands hung limp. We saw you die.

It's been so long since you were here,
and all is dry as ash, consumable.
Weep for yourselves, and not for me
—but do you feel our love grow cold and still?
Teach us to weep, to wake from sleep,
to think of you up on that hill.

The wood is dry, and everywhere
men beat their breasts and call for rocks to fall
and women cry and tear their hair;
yet hardly any turn to you; they all
would curse your name, give you the blame—
and drink the bitter cup of gall.

In the greenness of your return,
the parched ones, dry as sin, will be consumed.
And all that cannot last will burn,
and what was buried then will be exhumed.
Whose love remains in spite of pain
will rise like flames to be with you.

A Deeper Knowing

Only wonder leads to knowing.
~ ST. GREGORY OF NYSSA

The rocks and trees speak to us, but we do not understand them.
~ CZESŁAW MIŁOSZ

Quiddity

A bird must be known this way:
breathe with the flock as it lifts, settles.

Gaze down on haloed heads,
ribbon rivers, the geometric plain;

feel thermals sifting feathers,
air down the bone's hollow.

Rejoice in the provision
of the daily worm.

In this way you will inhabit
not just the bird

but your own life.
You'll know the sum

that out-glorifies
parts, function, need.

You'll learn to praise distinctions—
will find yourself

giddy, whispering names:
chickadee, junco, redwing.

Just Before

When Jesus comes again
in all his glory, somewhere in
the Sichuan mountains tires will crackle
over corn spread out on the road—
easy threshing—while a small child
urinates in the gutter, absorbed
in watching the car shoot by.

As the first rent opens
a fingernail tear in the hazy sky,
a woman in the foothills above Rishikesh
will lay down her firewood burden
and light the clay Diwali lamp
in the chilling dusk
circling her cupped hands in blessing.

In the pause before the clamor
of heaven's trumpets,
the jurors' waiting room in Baltimore's
civic court will throb with the quiet
turning of pages, a buzzing phone
in the hand of a tired man, berating
himself for forgetting to bring coffee.

Just before we are aware of him,
Jesus will pause to survey the view;
two shepherd boys amidst boulders
in the Wadi Rum hills south of Amman
wipe sleep from their eyes and stand amazed
at the blood-red poppies at their feet
stretching to the eastern horizon.

The Truth about the River

Perhaps we had it
backward.

Perhaps the canyon
shaped the river—

she, struggling in his hard
embrace, flailing every which

way, searching wild and white-eyed
for the fastest way home.

Perhaps she didn't cut
through him, boldly,

ignoring his cries,
carving scars that remain

beautiful, watermarks
on red walls.

Instead, it was he
channeling her through

his body of silt,
flesh and stone,

peeling off her layers of sediment
gradually, marking them

against his ribs as he took her
deeper into himself.

Dream

We were held captive, were being sorted.

Most of us were given a choice: some indistinct camp
or Great Lavra: an ancient monastery, a remote steppe.

I knew that was the place, though winter was beginning.
We might be able to scavenge (they said) for food, for kindling.

As we arrived, a late and weak sun shone blue on the snow.
At my feet in a basket: five baby chicks already stiff with frost.

It felt like the end of the world—the end of everything.

I feared, then, the coming hardship; knew some of us
would not see spring. Yet the displaced monks

made room for us, swept aside piles of books, papers;
thinned their soup, put out more bowls in loving silence.

This was a holy place: I understood we would suffer
whatever came with the monks. The snow on the ground

was blue; the light was fading. We were too many, too ill-clad.
I was afraid—yet not afraid. The monks made room for us.

When I woke up, I wanted to return.

Walk to Emmaus

But we had hoped
this paper life,

these shadow lands,
might be fleshed out,

thickened into
themselves—

at the very least
illumined by

far-spaced
signal fires.

We lean into the stranger:
moist lion's breath

now chilling,
now warming.

Small flame flares
open in the breast.

We press mystery:
remain with us.

Dry loaf breaks—
an instant's light!

Our great desire
vanishes,

leaving us kindled,
shalom rounder

on our tongues,
all that was hollow

now hallowed,
telling and retelling—

did not our hearts
burn?

Mali at Ramadan

>   Karachi, Pakistan

Across the elementary field
of brownish-green grass
where I'm playing horses

with friends, I see the *mali*
wetting his lips with the hose.
It's noon, and Ramadan,

and the day is hot. I wonder
if I'm witnessing a transgression.
I wonder if it matters.

Mali means gardener in Urdu.

By Degrees

You write our lives like Dostoevsky writes
his novels—gorgeous, unwieldy, spinning
out in various threads, but held together, tight
and centered, by a luminous vision,

forever always just out of our sight,
though we catch glimpses enough to keep us
coming back. Like in your stories—the light
lit by the woman with the lost coin sweeps us

in its beam: we rake the dirt beside her,
watch her mouth moving as she prays, presses
earth-warm silver to her lips—the finder
finds what matters most. In the midst of mess

you wait, content, for years—decades even—
for all your stories to settle and shape
within us, till we come to see each scene
as something to inhabit, and we wake

to more than morals, wake to mysteries
that root in us—the kingdom by degrees.

Metanoia

Whatever else he was,
        or had done,
it took a child
        to climb the tree—

it's a child's face
        Christ sees
through the leaves.

Allegory

He has left the shore,
mainland bound—
and already I wonder
at our grief: our teeth
biting against the awful
itch of island fever,
souls twitching under
fragile skin, envy and fear
coursing our veins—

the one almost plunging us
into the waves, the other
tethering our wild,
leaping hearts to this
blasted earth.

This Givenness

> "All of the small, old things." ~ Paul Kingsnorth

In morning's first light I'm arrested
by the depth of the dining table:
the warm, rough grooves satisfy and prick
an unspecified longing, one I stoke
as I fuss with zinnias, photograph them
against the rich grain.

                    I put down my phone
and wonder: Do we have enough candles
for the coming dark? What do we need
to recover that we used to know, if
it all falls apart, so we can start
again? Could I locate an almanac,
or navigate by stars? Distinguish
which wild herbs can be eaten? And why
does the sight, the touch, of this deep wood
compel a fear that feels somehow healthy—
as if I were a novice seer?

If I want to warm my body in wool,
to know the chill of moving from the hearth—
if I want to see again moisture
beading the inside of window panes,
or clothes on the line out back—is this
nostalgia or prophecy?

                    Something
whispers, urgent: we have need of stone
masons, wrought iron, terracotta,
keepers of bees. Some (artists, with their
antennae) tremble at this already.
They also secretly rejoice. This is
not sentiment. It's returning.

                    It's there
for the knowing—in linen, humus,
clay, leather, birch—though we've grown hard of
seeing their engendered shalom, how they
bless by circumscribing a human span
to all our days.
                    May we recover this.

One Unused to Ashes

2020

It grew in me throughout the day:
an urgency for lament,

the marking of sorrow onto my flesh,
a general confession.

So that evening, I stole into
an unfamiliar sanctuary.

There were few of us: strangers,
but not altogether so.

The ceiling was high and far away,
the room cold.

How quickly we were invited
to come, to kneel:

*Remember you are dust,
and to dust you shall return.*

I praised the *memento mori*,
the ashes gritty and warm.

My body needed that double trip
to the altar, that bending of the knee.

The body of Christ, broken for you.
The blood of Christ, shed for you.

Somehow, that cross has remained
these many months

a weightless burden,
an easy yoke.

It Is Happening Now (I)

Rain has been falling for so many days
(all records have been broken by now),
we are past remarking on its duration,
severity, and cumulative effects.

Our senses are dulled to the gentle hum
of the dehumidifier, slow creep
of water into walls, dark scent of rot—
even though it's steadily worsening,

even though if the deluge continues
it could bring this house down in ruin.
We're past perceiving, past imagining
how a single drop of rain rushing earth

contains in itself a thousand rainbows,
the sea and everything in it, its skin
supple and pulsing with limestone and silt—
ancient mountains falling gently down.

It Is Happening Now (II)

> But artists' antennae pick up every wave; and they suffered,
> surprised that they did so.
> ~ Czesław Miłosz

Brother,

Refuse the pillow placed beneath your head.

Decide now: while the lights remain on
and the cupboards are half-full and your neighbor
neither fears nor watches you.

Slip the net, the noose, the flag-draped box.
Choose exile now: before only two options remain.

Accustom yourself to being wooed and shamed—
for so they treated the prophets.

In writing this, I have sealed my fate.

Post-Miracle (I)

After the miracle
I made soup.

It felt ridiculous, but what
could I do?

We still needed to eat.

My daughter could not walk.
For months.

Then she did,
following a stranger's prayer.

I followed her around the house,
believing and

disbelieving my eyes.
I cried.

She took a shower, then,
because she could.

I was alone.
I knelt in the living room.

I believe. Help my unbelief.

*Depart from me, Lord—
I am sinful.*

This is what Peter cries
after his miracle catch of fish.

I get it now.

No one else tells you
how strange, how empty-handed

you feel. The fear
of stewarding this great thing.

The urge to return quickly
to familiarity. To soup.

Post-Miracle (II)

Was it my fault—my faith too weak—
my daughter's healing didn't last?
I don't know what to do with that.
Does it now undo everything?

It sometimes seems a sleight of hand,
a mystery, a bitter trick.
In rage I want to raise my fist—
or at the least, to understand.

The scriptures show us just the times
the hand was healed, the sight restored,
the joy of our compassionate Lord
as he turned water into wine,

the years of blood stopped at a word—
but did she never bleed again?
Was that the last of any pain
she felt in life? Likewise, we've heard

about the widow's son who sat
amazed, upright on his own bier.
His grave is with us still somewhere,
we must assume. So, is it that

we just be grateful for the few
months of reprieve, the added years
we get, exchanged for postponed tears?
The balance that we owe comes due

on down the line? Or could it be
that this is how we learn to pray?
We know he gives and takes away.
We raise our faces as we grieve

a fresh wound or a mortal blow,
the miracle forgotten now.
We say yes to the pain and how
it comes after the healing goes.

The Interior

October
Body songs of crickets pulse into the open window
on a cool current, and all of us in the house
go quiet at the coming change, when these songs
will go silent, one by one; when the bark
leaches its heat, gives up a little more each day,
gives in to the long sleep; when the crows return
and huddle in branch tops, black against the vesper light.

My long-limbed daughter approaches my height—
how much I have to hold close now, for her.
Her body song pleads in myriad ways, *Let me stay hidden.*
It's time now to buffer her, to bite my tongue:
she owns her own stories, anecdotes, shame.
I didn't expect this turn inward, this closing.

November
Snow geese blanket the banks by the lake. All else
feels pared down to essence, which is the work of autumn:
the welcome shivering-off of excess, trappings.
Summer's expanse reverses itself, contracting
to meet our need for a season of muffled sounds,
of dimly lit rooms, flickering light, and shadow.

The earth closes herself up for a while, so we follow
her lead inside, huddling close in fleece blankets,
cupping mugs in chilled hands. There we rediscover
the scratch of vinyl spinning songs we'd forgotten
in the bright, brash summer; early blue-gold twilight;
steaming soup and bread. Through long evenings, we begin
to see each other anew. Sharp edges soften.

December
In fire glow and shadow, she sits under my wing;
cocooned, she ventures voicing her fears in whispers.
I paint back to her a vision: strength, radiance,
a body and soul at peace. My hope is that in here,
words will feel weightier, easier to believe.

What I mean to say comes out right.
It hangs between us, crystalizes—a snowflake
she stretches out her hand to catch. Silently, I pray
that it has staying power, that she will carry it with her
into tomorrow's frozen dawn, intact, glowing.

January
It's safe in here, but the time is coming when doors
and windows will fling open to warming breezes
blowing every direction. This is mostly good.
We will turn out, tumble out, laugh at ourselves in
the overwhelming sunshine, be pulled along by
the wind. The turning inside-out will leave us raw,

frightened, exhilarated. What essential thing
will she take with her from this chrysalis season?
Will she trust her body, mind, heart, words
when exposed once again to the sun's expansive glare?
Tonight, she reads a novel next to the fire. Smiles
when I bring her tea in a china cup.
Waits, warms, strengthens.

Chengdu Pastoral

Sichuan, China

I'm in love with early morning,   but not here:
the thin, breakable blue skim of sky   I glimpse
between the spears of cement palisades   over my head
transports me to that other extreme: that same brittle blue breaking
over the Cotswolds,   solitary bundles of sheep
herding wisps of fog haltingly   up the limestone slopes
toward the slow simmer   of dawn, all soundless
and hushed. I see it, hear it: a distant cowbell,
(not the harsh warble of the *baozi* vendor   heating propane
on his bicycle's trailer on the sidewalk)   a cable-knitted figure
emerging with unhurried purpose from   the kitchen door
of the farmhouse, pauses,   lifts his head and his mug, breathes.

The steaming buns plop   into my plastic bag
and the vendor grins at me. *Zao!*   *Morning!* Yes, I am early;
it is early morning. And there is   blue in the sky
today. Even here.

Cicadas, East of Eden

Sichuan, China

Mid-summer, I crested the ridge of the hill behind
my flat, the bare brown shoulder rising naked
above its garment of summer growth and encroaching
city. My breath hummed with the music of the full sun
as an iridescent body magnetized my eyes to itself:
skewered by the sun's full rays against a dry trunk,
it heaved and accordioned itself in and out, up and down.
I leaned in, not breathing because of the power of that voice
that is not even a voice, how it could consume the span
of earth and sky and then cease, leaving
everything shaken, changed.

Before, I never searched them out, unnerved
by the sheer terror of that volume, sounding like
everything in the world, threatening to blast me
off my feet—then swallowing into sudden silence.
I averted my eyes when trapped in that screeching
bubble of space. Now, I hungered to know
everything about them: spider-veined transparent wings,
tymbals contracting to amplify sound through a hollow
abdomen, such that permanent hearing loss could occur
if it were right next to your ear.

The Chinese have a saying: *shedding the golden
cicada skin*—escaping danger by using deception
or decoy, because of the empty husks left behind,
clinging to the bark of trees. Or the repeated shedding
of illusions until what is real is left. The last time

I saw one up close was early fall, festival time downtown,
and a giggling, mini-skirted young woman thrust
a wooden skewer into my son's hand. The magnificent body
was pierced through and scorched.

I held my breath and he held his arm out away
and we both flinched when a leg moved. My gaze spun
around the square—the cruel lollipops in hands everywhere—
and I remembered I had read China is one of the many
places where cicadas are eaten. My son rushed after her,
mumbling *wo bu yao—I don't want it*—and he wiped his eyes
and grabbed my hand. *I want to go home*, he said.
And we left, and what was left with me is this:
that we all keep failing utterly
at our original vocation.

A Prayer: On Synthetic Snowflakes

An electron microscope brings to light our failure:
our creative powers truncated into gob-like flakes
too dense to dance, the dull dream of a hollow core.

These flakes lack the hexagonal balance of the real
whirl and whorl. We've seen it—symmetry so intricate
we gasp in delight; crystals branching from the surprise

of a dust-mote centerpiece; rime ice caught in mid-
pirouette against cold glass. Have we lost the capacity
to marvel at this complexity? To praise, even, the dark center

melting against our skin? (The familiar ache: all we touch
reduces—edges flat, blurred.) So we come to ask:
crystalize our stilted imaginations, our flat souls.

Acedia

> "And he gave them their request; but sent leanness into their soul." Psalm 106:15 (KJV)

Our arms, they feel like lead; the spoon slips back
into the bowl; its weight too much to bear.
But did we really want the soup at all?
It stuffs our bellies sick, that's all; because
desire's edges have been cauterized,
we hardly know when we've been satisfied.
In fact, the satisfaction feels so thin.
Our heavy eyelids, limpid limbs can't strive
or wait or sacrifice, can't bear the weight
of living—nothing's worth the hassle now
or worth the cost in time or sweat or love.
And in our ear the whine of *Is this all?*
Yes, is this all there is? We find no strength
to slap at the mosquito in our ear.
We're granted what we think we wanted, but
we pay with souls that are dis-eased; we're lost
and harried every day, distracted. Yet
that hum—it's lurking always in the back
of memory (the bit we haven't yet
destroyed or labeled as nostalgia)—says
You're sick—and now and then another one
explodes, and no one says *We're sick, that's why*
the gun, the bomb, the knife, the chosen death.
It must all be taboo, and so we smirk,
because today there's nothing holy left.
At least, there's nothing worth so much we'd want
to change our habits, pleasures, license for.

It's like a thin and poisoned vapor cools
the center of our hearts, the inner life
we held in common once, distinct in all
its diverse beauty and varieties—
the part that thrilled to all the old and deep
imaginations, poems, prayers, and songs,
the store of wisdom passed along the way.
We've thinned ourselves—our very selves—and now
the mist asphyxiates, our senses dull,
and we can't bring ourselves to care, or weep
for all that we've forgotten, left behind.
And we've lost more than we can ever hope
to gain again. We find our love grown cold.

Everything Is a Departure

The words have left my mouth;
the food is snaking down, taste whispering away.

You're closing the magazine; I'm calculating
the tip. Just like the rain that turned

to suffocating steam on pavement,
our city sunk a quarter-inch last year

into the bay while nobody noticed.

The shark they tagged is gone
to deeper depths, out of our zone.

Monarchs started out weeks early
for their southern climes, surprising

no one but those who were watching.
The Koreas disconnected phone lines,

and we read it with inevitability
in the morning news.

Today I longed to speak to an operator
whose fingers would connect

my vocal vibrations to someone
who was waiting for them.

I looked for landlines in each store we passed,
irritating you with my weighted walk.

I can't comprehend the cloud:
it's a figment—isn't it?

Somewhere there must be something
not winding down, not racing toward oblivion

or planned obsolescence: a warm voice
that won't surrender to a dial tone. Instead,

breath on our ear. Wonder will surprise us again,
though we'd forgotten: orange fish mouthing at us

from an undulating surface we can touch,
pages made of trees fluttering open,

screens blank and cracked—nothing left to say.
Language lengthening again, mouthed.

No more curbside drop-offs—we'll be allowed
the kiss at the gate once more.

Cairn at West Clear Creek

Just past the first stream crossing,
an astonishing little altar—

that meant someone stooped low
to gather stones,

ones that lie flat and heavy
in the palm.

A benevolent hand
arranged them, one after the other,

measuring by feel
a balance that could endure

wild wet and wind
and still point the way—

someone who knew
there would come along

those whose stones
had all been scattered.

Clarification

I.

The wind today stole all the joy of life—
set marrow trembling in these aging bones,
found all she sought with her hungry knife,
filled every hidden hollow with her moans.

There was no escaping from her grip—
she cut and cut till I emerged from stone.
I arrived at journey's end strafed and stripped,
riddled through with air and light, undone.

II.

The lake's face is all jagged white caps:
clarity only achieved on the coldest
of days, thin wind scouring the sky,

a faint, curved winter moon, quiet
as a forgotten scar—it seems to shift,
appears now here, now there.

Bone-bare limbs of trees, dull and resigned,
can't compare to the urgent beauty
of brittle beaks, sharp wingtips

of gulls drifting, shocked still, on the water—
wind lifting and lowering them
while fish dive deeper underneath.

III.
I lean into the gale because
I know this secret: in the death
of winter, when trees brace themselves
against blasts that shatter the sky,
they are secretly composing
the white poems that, months later,
they will cup in greening hands.

Speak Like Rain

> Kikuyu farm youth to Karen Blixen, after listening to
> her recite poetry

Speak like rain, sister,
those smooth, plump drops that beat
water-rhythm on our chests—
words shaped like the curve
of an ear, the cup above the lobe—

fill it again.

Speak again; the rain
has been too long in coming
and this scorched sod waits;
words flew on wings and
summoned the plovers hunting

for new grass.

Speak like rain—play
those tricks with light and clouds,
hope and dry madness;
words that smell far away,
like the sea, drifted here just now,

tasting of salt.

Late Discovery

I came home to November
               in my late thirties—
child of deserts
       (lizards, dried mung bean pods,
      rubber sandals stuck to hot tar)

and tropics
       (monsoon rains pounding a tin roof,
     low clouds like gauze in my mouth,
       skitter of roaches
            when the light is flipped).

Cold November is welcome
      mystery: half-lit
        mix of blaze and gray,
     lonely in the best sense
of the word;

moonstone sky,
    gnarled and naked trees
        flinging claws up against
lava sunsets.

Introverted, November
      makes no demands:
swirls around my ankles
   (leaves or fog),

sings in a minor key,
    needs tea in the afternoon,
fewer words.

Roundtop Ski Lodge

    for Collin

He skis in short sleeves.
The wind picks up; blue clouds

against a sinking March sun.
He glides down, rides up—

pause, breath, silence.
On the lift, his slim form is slack.

He inhales the last threads of color, sky;
anticipates the skim down in the blue dark.

At the top he leans into solitude,
into the wind,

savors how the moguls rise
in relief against shadow.

Cusp

The word I'm rolling around
in my mouth today, testing its
diving lip, is *cusp*.

Its smoothness startles,
sweeps over an unseen edge,
a natural progression.

Cusp: both an ending and
a starting point, but lacking
a point's sharpness.

Instead, it curves over—
a waterfall, a joyous dive.
I imagine the possibilities:

a deep blue pool, a splash,
then a strenuous, satisfying swim
for new shores.

Gravity and Grace

> for Collin, after Simone Weil

You take a running lunge at the side
of the tunnel slide, slap yourself over it
like a wet dishrag, slide slowly down,
and land in a lump on smooth pebbles.
Your tongue hangs out of a silly grin,
your eyes cross, and I imagine cartoon birds
circling with stars over your head.

You sit on the rug for an hour,
folding origami dinosaurs, teaching me
distinguishing attributes of each species.
You approve my choice of Mendelssohn
on the turntable and tell me you like
this time with me. I iron and you fold,
and outside it rains, and keeps raining.

You list all the reasons why we should
get a low-maintenance dog. You've done
your research. And when I hint you might
have to wait until you're out on your own,
you walk slowly up the stairs, reciting "Harlem"
from memory, shutting your door softly,
dramatically, on *or does it explode?*

Late February

A hazy potential hovers about
the dogwoods and early magnolias.
Almost unnoticed, they cloud into blossom.

These are the days of firsts: crocus, robin,
tulip leaf. A week or two and we'll stop
remarking, then noticing—until all

is riot and wind and March abundance
and whispering: you can reorder your
closet, kitchen, office, life. We'll pretend

not to hear—something in us recoils from
enacting a cliché. We'll avoid talk
of how it all lifts (is meant to lift?) us,

cleans our gaze, teases us with hope we might—
what, exactly? And why? Doesn't it go
just like this every year? We won't be fools.

We freeze back into winter's last embrace,
smirk at our sappy selves. The trees hold their
applause and stifle a deep-rooted groan.

My Daughter Asks for a Pomegranate

At first I hurried: cut the fruit in half
the wrong direction, used a spoon to scoop
out seeds that scattered everywhere; the fruit
resisted my untrained advance. I laughed
and slowed my pace and settled to the task:
thumbs coaxing gently through the sponge to root
the arils out (I threw aside the spoon).
Contented, mesmerized, I hunted, basked
in hidden glory bursting forth, that stained
my fingertips, the cutting board, the bowl.
The fleshy mesocarp lay broken, slain—
until just then, I hadn't cared to know
how slow love is, and what the parts are named.

Notes

Bright Sadness, Bitter Joy—The epigraph for the first section of this collection is a quote from an interview with poet Ilya Kaminsky. The article is titled "Still Dancing: An Interview with Ilya Kaminsky," and it was published in the 2019 March/April issue of *Poets & Writers Magazine*. Garth Greenwell was the interviewer.

"Remnants of Empire"—The Hindi word *ayah* designates a female domestic worker or caregiver, especially in European households in India.

"Philoxenia"—The word *philoxenia* is Greek for "love of the stranger."

"Disaster Chaplaincy Training"—Our instructor for a disaster chaplaincy training course I took referenced Henri Nouwen's *The Wounded Healer: A Story of Homecoming* (Doubleday, 1979). Nouwen believed that people who minister to others in suffering must have an awareness of the suffering in their own hearts.

"High Winds on the Chesapeake Bay Bridge"—The italicized words in the poem are from Frederick Buechner's sermon-essay "The Magnificent Defeat" in *Secrets in the Dark: A Life in Sermons* (Harper San Francisco, 2006).

"Visit to Sarajevo"—The quoted and italicized words in the poem are taken directly from signs posted in Sarajevo, one at the tunnel museum and one at the city's library.

"Accumulated Lessons in Displacement"—When I was fourteen, my family and other foreigners were evacuated from Kinshasa, Democratic Republic of the Congo, following a week of violent rioting and looting of the city by soldiers and civilians fed up with corrupt government and skyrocketing inflation. That experience of abrupt displacement—coupled with my life as a global nomad—gives me a deeper empathy for others who have been displaced. This poem grew out of my own lessons learned, the experiences of dear Bosnian refugee friends, and stories I'd read of Syrian refugees' experiences over the last few years. It takes the long view, looking at what settles, what emerges, what remains, and what connects or distances us from one another in displacement.

"Kou"—This Mandarin Chinese word means "mouth." The Chinese character for it resembles a square, which is meant to symbolize an open mouth. "Ji kou ren" is part of a common question, "Ni jia you ji kou ren," which means, "How many people are in your household?" The more literal meaning translates to "How many mouths do you have to feed?"

"The Morning After Freddie Gray's Funeral"—I began writing this poem while our city was on lockdown following civil unrest in response to the death of Freddie Gray, who suffered fatal injuries to his cervical spinal cord while in police custody on April 12, 2015. None of the six officers believed to be involved in his death were ultimately held accountable for Gray's death. The majority of our neighbors where we lived at that time were African American.

"The Wood Is Dry"—Jesus's italicized words in this poem come from Luke 23:28–31.

A Deeper Knowing—One of the epigraphs for the second section of this collection is a quote from an essay by Czesław Miłosz titled "Introduction to Stanislaw Vincenz, On the Side of Memory," from *Beginning with My Streets: Essays and Recollections* (Farrar, Straus, and Giroux, 1991).

"Quiddity"—*Quiddity* is the essential nature of a thing. The *quiddity* of a thing is greater than the sum of its parts, greater than its physical characteristics. (G. K. Chesterton playfully described the "horseness" of a horse when discussing this concept and how it relates to our understanding of reality.)

"Dream"—I wrote down the details of this vivid dream soon after waking, and it assembled itself into this poem quicky and almost effortlessly (this is not usually the case).

"This Givenness"—The epigraph is a quote from an interview with Paul Kingsnorth for *Front Porch Republic*. The article was titled "Spiritual Secession: A Conversation with Paul Kingsnorth," November 12, 2021. Jeffrey Bilbro was the interviewer.

"It Is Happening Now (II)"—The epigraph for this poem is a quote by Czesław Miłosz from his memoir *Native Realm: A Search for Self-Definition* (English edition, Farrar, Straus, and Giroux, 2002).

"Post-Miracle (I)" and "Post-Miracle (II)"—From one moment to the next, after a prayer, my daughter was once miraculously healed of complex regional pain syndrome (CRPS), a beast of a nerve condition nicknamed "the suicide disease" because it causes off-the-charts nerve pain and it has no cure. I wrote "Post-Miracle (I)" a day or two after the healing (at the time, it was just titled "Post-Miracle"). After two glorious months free of pain, my daughter's CRPS came back. Hence, "Post-Miracle (II)." We never know the end of our stories. We're grateful that after intensive, outside-of-the-box treatment, her CRPS has been in full remission for four years and counting.

"Acedia"—*Acedia* (Greek) is a vice often referred to as "The Noonday Devil"; it is also variously known as sloth, despair, indifference, hatred of life and of the good, etc. It encompasses a vague and anxious restlessness, sadness and despair, a lack of interest or care in life or others, loss of interest in spiritual things, a sense of torpor and listlessness, an inability to be alone without distractions, idle curiosity, and general dissatisfaction. In general, acedia flattens and thins out life. It renders everything meaningless.

"Speak Like Rain"—The title of this poem is a sentence that Kikuyu farm youth on Karen Blixen's (pen name Isak Dinesen) farm in Kenya said to her when she recited poetry to them. The encounter is related in her memoir, *Out of Africa*.

"Gravity and Grace"—The title of this poem refers to a book by the same name by philosopher Simone Weil. She wrote about modernity's severing of earth and heaven—the gravitational pull of earthly things and the opposing grace of longing for God. Weil also spoke of "metaxu," which are moments of human experience that function as a bridge between the material and the spiritual, between earth and heaven.

About the Poet

Rachel E. Hicks's poems, essays, and short fiction have been published in various journals. She has been nominated for the Pushcart Prize three times, and her short story "Drink It Dry" won the 2019 Briar Cliff Review Fiction Prize. She is the assistant editor of *Mars Hill Audio* and the former editor of *Among Worlds*, a publication for global nomads. Rachel was born in the foothills of the Himalayas and spent the bookends of her childhood in India, with moves to Pakistan, Jordan, the Democratic Republic of the Congo, the United States, and Hong Kong in between. As an adult she has lived in Phoenix, Arizona, and Chengdu, China. She currently lives with her husband in Baltimore, Maryland, and she has two adult children. This is her debut poetry collection.

www.ingramcontent.com/pod-product-compliance
Lightning Source LLC
Chambersburg PA
CBHW061451040426
42450CB00007B/1310